HISTORY IN PICTURES

FOCUS ON
THE GREAT
MIGRATION

DR. ARTIKA R. TYNER

Lerner Publications ◆ Minneapolis

LETTER FROM CICELY LEWIS

Dear Reader,

Imagine being in an argument with a classmate and the teacher asks what happened. Your classmate tells their version of the story, but you don't get to share your version. Do you think this is fair? Well, this is what has happened throughout history.

CICELY LEWIS

This series looks at different events in US history with a focus on photos that help tell stories of people from underrepresented groups.

I started the Read Woke challenge in response to the needs of my students. I wanted my students to read books that challenged social norms and shared perspectives from underrepresented and oppressed groups. I created Read Woke Books because I want you to be knowledgeable and compassionate citizens.

As you look through these books, think about the photos that have captured history. Why are they important? What do they teach you? I hope you learn from these books and get inspired to make our world a better place for all.

Yours in solidarity,

—Cicely Lewis, Executive Editor

TABLE OF CONTENTS

Think critically about the photos throughout this book. Who is taking the photos and why? What is their viewpoint? Who are the people in the photos? What do these photos tell us?

There are so many important people and events in the Great Migration, and we are not able to include them all in this book. After finishing this book, learn how you can get involved. There are tips on page 25 to help you get started.

This family left the South for Chicago in 1920.

NEW BEGINNINGS

HUMAN MIGRATION IS A JOURNEY OF DISCOVERY. It focuses on discovering a pathway to the future. Some people migrate for better housing, jobs, education, and even access to health care. Others seek to build new communities and neighborhoods together. Each chapter of a family's migration journey is about seeking better opportunities for the next generation.

The Great Migration (1916–1970) offered this hope for the Black community. Economic freedom and the promise of liberty were an inspiration for this journey. After slavery, many Black people moved to cities for more opportunities. Some moved east to Philadelphia, others relocated west to California, and some left the United States, moving to places such as Haiti, Mexico, Liberia, and Canada. They were also leaving behind terrible situations. They faced racial violence, sharecropping, and more. Black people envisioned a pathway to racial equality. With hard work and determination, Black people were determined to build a prosperous future for generations to come.

About six million Black people moved during the Great Migration.

From 1500 to the mid-1800s, the Transatlantic slave trade kidnapped millions of Africans and forced them into enslavement in the US.

CHAPTER 1
FREEDOM FROM SLAVERY

DURING THE TRANSATLANTIC SLAVE TRADE, WHITE ENSLAVERS KIDNAPPED, ENSLAVED, AND FORCED AFRICANS TO THE UNITED STATES. White enslavers treated Black people like chattel property and not human beings. Black people built the economy of America through their blood, sweat, and tears. They worked in the fields under grueling conditions. They cultivated cotton, tobacco, sugarcane, and rice. With each generation, they kept their eye on the promised land of freedom. Many believed this meant they were destined to follow the North Star and seek freedom from bondage. They hoped to find refuge in the North.

The Civil War (1861–1865) was waged between the North (Union) and South (Confederacy). Tensions between the North and South were fueled by the debate over whether or not to abolish slavery. Enslaved people were the laborers in the fields, farms, and businesses. The rebelling states of the Confederacy did not want to lose their free labor.

The Thirteenth Regiment was a group of Black men who fought for the North during the Civil War.

In 1862 President Abraham Lincoln issued the Emancipation Proclamation declaring all enslaved people in the Confederate states would be free on January 1, 1863. This served as a turning point for the Black community in the South. Thousands fled from the South to join the Union army. Enslaved people had to fight for their freedom since the proclamation didn't do it. There were also enslaved people in the Union states. The proclamation did not free them.

Over 180,000 Black people fought for the Union. Some were fighting for their own freedom, while some insisted on their right to fight. Black people helped the Union to win the Civil War. The famous abolitionist Frederick Douglass worked hard to recruit Black soldiers. He believed serving the military would provide the Black community with a pathway to full citizenship.

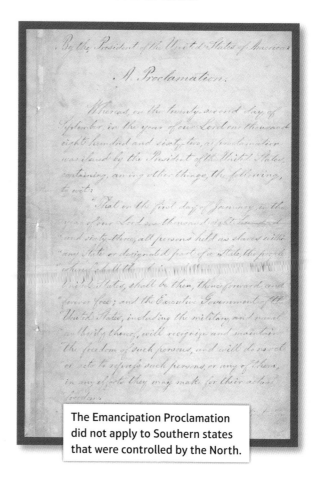

The Emancipation Proclamation did not apply to Southern states that were controlled by the North.

TO COLORED MEN!

FREEDOM,

Protection, Pay, and a Call to Military Duty!

On the 1st day of January, 1863, the President of the United States proclaimed FREEDOM to over THREE MILLIONS OF SLAVES. This decree is to be enforced by all the power of the Nation. On the 21st of July last he issued the following order:

PROTECTION OF COLORED TROOPS.

"WAR DEPARTMENT, ADJUTANT GENERAL'S OFFICE,
WASHINGTON, July 21.

"General Order, No. 233.

"The following order of the President is published for the information and government of all concerned:—

EXECUTIVE MANSION, WASHINGTON, July 30.

'"It is the duty of every Government to give protection to its citizens, of whatever class, color, or condition, and especially to those who are duly organized as soldiers in the public service. The law of nations, and the usages and customs of war, as carried on by civilized powers, permit no distinction as to color in the treatment of prisoners of war as public enemies. To sell or enslave any captured person on account of his color, is a relapse into barbarism, and a crime against the civilization of the age.

'"The Government of the United States will give the same protection to all its soldiers, and if the enemy shall sell or enslave any one because of his color, the offense shall be punished by retaliation upon the enemy's prisoners in our possession. It is, therefore, ordered, for every soldier of the United States, killed in violation of the laws of war, a rebel soldier shall be executed; and for every one enslaved by the enemy, or sold into slavery, a rebel soldier shall be placed at hard labor on the public works, and continued at such labor until the other shall be released and receive the treatment due to prisoners of war.

'"ABRAHAM LINCOLN."'

'"By order of the Secretary of War.

'"E. D. TOWNSEND, Assistant Adjutant General."'

That the President is in earnest the rebels soon began to find out, as witness the following order from his Secretary of War:

"WAR DEPARTMENT, WASHINGTON CITY, August 8, 1863.

"SIR: Your letter of the 3d inst., calling the attention of this Department to the cases of Orin H. Brown, William H. Johnston, and Wm. Wilson, three colored men captured on the gunboat Isaac Smith, has received consideration. This Department has directed that three rebel prisoners of South Carolina, if there be any such in our possession, and if not, three others, be confined in close custody and held as hostages for Brown, Johnston and Wilson, and that the fact be communicated to the rebel authorities at Richmond.

"Very respectfully your obedient servant,

"EDWIN M. STANTON, Secretary of War.

"The Hon. GIDEON WELLES, Secretary of the Navy."

And retaliation will be our practice now—man for man—to the bitter end.

LETTER OF CHARLES SUMNER,

Written with reference to the Convention held at Poughkeepsie, July 15th and 16th, 1863, to promote Colored Enlistments.

BOSTON, July 13th, 1863.

"I doubt if, in times past, our country could have expected from colored men any patriotic service. Such service is the return for protection. But now that protection has begun, the service should begin also. Nor should relative rights and duties be weighed with nicety. It is enough that our country, aroused at last to a sense of justice, seeks to enrol colored men among its defenders.

"If my counsels should reach such persons, I would say: enlist at once. Now is the day and now is the hour. Help to overcome your cruel enemies now battling against your country, and in this way you will surely overcome those other enemies hardly less cruel, here at home, who will still seek to degrade you. This is not the time to hesitate or to higgle. Do your duty to our country, and you will set an example of generous self-sacrifice which will conquer prejudice and open all hearts.

"Very faithfully yours,

"CHARLES SUMNER."

This flyer was posted to encourage Black men to join the North's military. Black people were referred as "colored" at the time, an offensive term. What do you think about this flyer? Is it fair that Black people had to fight for their freedom?

During the Civil War, Harriet Tubman gathered information from the South, led a raid, and more.

Harriet Tubman, known as the conductor of the Underground Railroad, served as a spy for the Union army. As she traveled throughout the South freeing enslaved Black people, she also led Union soldiers.

The Thirteenth Amendment abolished slavery throughout the US in 1865. An exception clause kept those convicted of a crime under the bondage of slavery.

JUNETEENTH

Not all states shared the announcement of the Emancipation Proclamation. In Galveston, Texas, it was not until June 19, 1865, that the entire Black community was freed. Troops came to enforce Black people's freedom. This date is celebrated every year as Juneteenth.

People march in a parade to celebrate Juneteenth in Pennsylvania in 2018.

During the 1919 Chicago Race Riot, white supremacists killed twenty-three Black people, injured hundreds, and burned down about one thousand Black families' homes.

CHAPTER 2

FREED BUT NOT FREE

ALTHOUGH **B**LACK PEOPLE WERE LEGALLY FREE, THEY STILL FACED MANY CHALLENGES. They needed economic power and safety from the threat of racial terrorism. White enslavers fought to keep their economic power by keeping their oppressive labor conditions. They also wanted to maintain their political power by ensuring the Black community could not vote. Laws were created to make sure racial segregation was a way of life. The case of *Plessy v.*

Ferguson (1896) declared that separate was equal, but things were rarely, if ever, equal. Black codes (1865–1866) and Jim Crow laws (1877–1965) ensured Black Americans would not have equal opportunities.

Lynchings and racial terrorism were also a constant threat. Between 1877 and 1950, white people lynched more than 4,440 Black people. White supremacists used vigilante violence to maintain their power. White mobs killed and brutalized the Black community.

Separate was not equal for Black people. Black schools often received fewer resources than white schools.

FREEDMAN'S SAVINGS BANK

Freedman's Savings Bank was established in 1865 to provide financial services to newly freed Black people. But in 1874, the bank closed, and $3 million (about $73.1 million in today's money) of people's life savings were lost and never returned. In 2016 the treasury secretary helped to rename the Treasury Annex Building on the site of the original Freedman's Savings Bank. Its name became the Freedman's Bank Building.

Freedman's Savings Bank standing in Washington, DC

A family moving away from Florida in 1940

Seeking the promise of liberty, justice, and pursuit of happiness, many Black people packed their belongings and left the South.

Before the Civil War, the majority of Black people in the US lived in the South. Starting in the early 1900s, millions of Black people migrated to the North, Midwest, and West, and some even left the United States.

> ## "To be a poor man is hard, but to be a poor race in a land of dollars is the very bottom of hardships."
>
> —W. E. B. Du Bois

A woman leaving Florida for a new job in North Carolina in 1940

CHAPTER 3
THE GUIDING NORTH STAR

DURING SLAVERY THE DREAM OF GOING NORTH MEANT FREEDOM FROM THE CHAINS OF BONDAGE SINCE MANY NORTHERN STATES HAD OUTLAWED SLAVERY. The freedom seekers went north. They looked for the North Star to illuminate the pathway to freedom.

From 1910–1930, many were guided on this journey. They left the fields of the South and sharecropping with hope for the future somewhere else. Some moved to larger metropolitan areas in the South, and some moved to the North. Those traveling North also wanted to leave the day-to-day realities of Jim Crow laws that limited access to jobs, housing, and even voting. Jim Crow laws ensured racial segregation. Migrants believed the North would live up to America's promise of equal rights and equal justice.

The Home Owners' Loan Corporation opened its offices in 1933. It used racist practices to deny Black people loans.

"ONE-WAY TICKET"

Poet and playwright Langston Hughes wrote about the migration experience. His poem "One-Way Ticket" focused on leaving injustices of the South behind such as Jim Crow laws and lynchings. He also wrote about the hope migrants had as they left the South for the West and North.

Hughes is known for his portrayal of Black life.

Black women make puttees, a cloth covering worn on the lower leg, in 1918.

During World War I (1914–1918), the North offered new jobs in factories and better wages. But it had its own set of challenges. Black people faced discrimination at work. They were paid less than white people. Schools in the Black community did not have the same access to resources. Communities were also under-resourced and segregated. Black people still faced barriers to freedom. Despite these challenges, many settled there and kept working toward building their family's legacy.

REFLECT

Black people are still paid less than white people for doing the same job. How do you think that has impacted Black people? What can be done to make payment more fair?

A boy sells the *Chicago Defender* newspaper in 1942.

NAB POLICE SLAYER MISSING 6 MONTHS

Chicago Defender

CHICAGOANS FIGHT

CHAPTER 4
BLACK CITIES AND BLACK HOPE

THE GREAT MIGRATION LED TO THE RAPID POPULATION GROWTH OF BLACK COMMUNITIES IN CITIES LIKE HARLEM, CHICAGO, AND DETROIT. Many migrated to Chicago after reading the *Chicago Defender*. The founder, Robert S. Abbott, migrated north from Georgia. His newspaper was an important resource in the Black community since it provided job postings and key resources for the migration journey.

Migration gave Black people the opportunity to create

wealth on their own terms. Black entrepreneurs developed new products and services while creating jobs. Lillian Harris Dean, "Pig Foot Mary," became wealthy by launching her own food truck. She sold pigs' feet on the streets of Harlem in a baby carriage.

The Black community still faces similar challenges. Racial terrorism like police brutality and vigilante danger is an ever-present threat. Black men are two and a half times more likely to be killed by the police compared to white men. Black people face violence for simply jogging or driving.

Diners sit in the Perfect Eat Shop, in Illinois in 1942. The Black-owned restaurant was run by Mr. and Mrs. Morris.

MADAM C. J. WALKER

Madam C. J. Walker created a line of hair care products and ran a beauty school. She employed forty thousand Black people to sell her products. She was the first Black woman to become a millionaire in the US.

Walker used her money to help others.

A Black Panther member serves free breakfasts to schoolchildren in 1969.

The Black community still faces high rates of poverty and unemployment. Nearly a quarter of Black families are in the third generation of poverty. Despite these barriers, the Black community is committed to building a pathway to success for future generations.

REFLECT

How can you make your community more welcoming to people who have historically been marginalized? How does your answer to this question depend on your status in society? In what ways is your community built for some people and not others?

Children jump rope in Chicago in the 1970s.

"Success is to be measured not so much by the position that one has reached in life as by the obstacles which he has overcome."

—Booker T. Washington

TAKE ACTION

Look at this map to learn more about the routes people took during the Great Migration:
https://kids.britannica.com/kids/assembly/view/247865.

Learn more about profiled leaders like Booker T. Washington, Harriet Tubman, and W. E. B. Du Bois.

Read about the 1919 Red Summer and 1921 Tulsa Race Massacre in Oklahoma.

Start or join a club about social justice.

Learn more about the Thirteenth Amendment and its impact on mass incarceration:
https://www.history.com/news/13th-amendment-slavery-loophole-jim-crow-prisons.

TIMELINE

1861–1865 The Civil War is waged between the North and South due to slavery.

1863 The Emancipation Proclamation is issued by President Lincoln. It declares that enslaved people in the Confederate states are free from slavery.

1865 The Thirteenth Amendment is passed, abolishing slavery except when a person is convicted of a crime.

1865 The Freedmen's Bureau is established by Congress under the Lincoln administration to educate and support the millions of newly freed Black people.

1865–1877 Reconstruction laws and policies are enacted after the Civil War to support the Black community with economic and political freedom.

1877–1965 Jim Crow laws in southern states enforce segregation among Black people and white people.

1910–1930 The First Great Migration occurs.

1940–1970 The Second Great Migration occurs, spurred on by industrialization.

PHOTO REFLECTION

The Tulsa Race Massacre took place from May 31 to June 1, 1921. A white mob attacked Black people and their community in Tulsa, Oklahoma. White people killed hundreds of Black people and destroyed their homes. Thousands of Black people were left unhoused.

What is the importance of knowing the history of the Tulsa massacre? What can be gained from excavating the past—and making sure that Tulsans and the rest of the country know what happened one hundred years ago?

How do you think this event should be remembered and memorialized? Should students learn about the massacre in schools? Should monuments, gathering places, and museums be dedicated to the victims and their descendants? What other ideas can you come up with?

GLOSSARY

ABOLITIONIST: a person who works to abolish an institution and practice

CHATTEL PROPERTY: tangible property that belongs to an individual

ENSLAVED: made into a slave; caused to lose freedom

JIM CROW LAWS: laws enacted by southern states post-Reconstruction to take away the rights of the Black community

MIGRATION: movement from one place to another

RACIAL TERRORISM: violent attacks on communities of color to stop economic, social, and political progress and maintain white supremacy

REFUGE: a condition of being safe from harm and danger

SHARECROPPING: when a landlord leases the land to a tenant in exchange for shares of the tenant's crops. Landlords often kept tenants in debt so they could make more money off the tenants.

WHITE SUPREMACIST: someone that believes that white people are superior and should have control over people of other races, such as Black people

SOURCE NOTES

15   W. E. B. Du Bois, *The Souls of Black Folk* (Chicago: A. C. McClurg, 1903), 8.

24   Booker T. Washington, *Up from Slavery: An Autobiography* (Garden City, NY: Doubleday, 1907), 39.

READ WOKE READING LIST

Britannica Kids: The Great Migration
https://kids.britannica.com/kids/article/Great-Migration
/632598

Britannica Kids: Tulsa Race Massacre of 1921
https://kids.britannica.com/kids/article/Tulsa-race-massacre
-of-1921/632653

History: The Great Migration
https://www.history.com/topics/black-history/great-migration

Imani, Blair. *Making Our Way Home: The Great Migration and the Black American Dream*. Emeryville, CA: Ten Speed, 2020.

Lewis, Cicely. *Mass Incarceration, Black Men, and the Fight for Justice*. Minneapolis: Lerner Publications, 2022.

PBS: The Great Migration
https://www.pbs.org/tpt/slavery-by-another-name/themes
/great-migration/

Weatherford, Carole Boston. *Unspeakable: The Tulsa Race Massacre*. Minneapolis: Carolrhoda Books, 2021.

Woodson, Jacqueline. *This Is the Rope: A Story from the Great Migration*. New York: Nancy Paulsen Books, 2013.

INDEX

PHOTO ACKNOWLEDGMENTS

Image credits: Everett Collection/Shutterstock.com, p. 4; AP Photo/Library of Congress/FSA/Russell Lee, p. 5; North Wind Picture Archives/Alamy Stock Photo, p. 6; Library of Congress, pp. 7, 10, 18, 20, 21; National Archives (299998), p. 8; National Archives, p. 9; Bastiaan Slabbers/Getty Images, p. 11; Everett Collection Historical/Alamy Stock Photo, p. 12; AP Photo/ Rudolph Faircloth, p. 13; SBS Eclectic Images/Alamy Stock Photo, pp. 14, 16; Everett Collection Historical/Alamy Stock Photo, p. 17; Stocktrek Images, Inc./Alamy Stock Photo, p. 19; Smithsonian Institution, National Museum of American History : Archives Center/Wikimedia Commons (public domain), p. 22; AP Photo/William Straeter, p. 23; National Archives (556160), p. 24; American Photo Archive/Alamy Stock Photo, p. 27; Cecily Lewis portrait photos by Fernando Decillis.

Cover: Library of Congress.

Content consultants: Peter Rachleff and Dr. Terry Anne Scott

Lerner Publications Company
An imprint of Lerner Publishing Group, Inc.
241 First Avenue North
Minneapolis, MN 55401 USA

For reading levels and more information, look up this title at www.lernerbooks.com.

Main body text set in Aptifer Sans LT Pro.
Typeface provided by Linotype AG.

Designer: Viet Chu
Lerner team: Martha Kranes

Library of Congress Cataloging-in-Publication Data

Names: Tyner, Artika R., author.
Title: Focus on the Great Migration / Dr. Artika R. Tyner.
Description: Minneapolis : Lerner Publications, 2023. | Series: History in pictures (read woke books) | Includes bibliographical references and index. | Audience: Ages 9–14 | Audience: Grades 4–6 | Summary: "During the Great Migration, a large number of Black Americans relocated when faced with segregation and poor economic conditions. While the places they moved to weren't free from racism, they fought for a better future"— Provided by publisher.
Identifiers: LCCN 2021051616 (print) | LCCN 2021051617 (ebook) | ISBN 9781728423494 (lib. bdg.) | ISBN 9781728462882 (pbk.) | ISBN 9781728461410 (eb pdf)
Subjects: LCSH: African Americans—Migrations—History—20th century—Juvenile literature. | Rural-urban migration—United States—History—20th century—Juvenile literature. | African Americans—History—1877–1964—Juvenile literature. | United States—Race relations—History—20th century—Juvenile literature.
Classification: LCC E185.6 .T96 2022 (print) | LCC E185.6 (ebook) | DDC 305.800973—dc23/eng/20211116

LC record available at https://lccn.loc.gov/2021051616
LC ebook record available at https://lccn.loc.gov/2021051617

Manufactured in the United States of America
1-49187-49318-3/14/2022